A Storm in a Shell - The Ebb and Flow of my Storm

by

Chel O' Hare

First published in Great Britain in 2025 by TEP Publishing

131 Finsbury Pavement, London EC2A 1NT

https://www.theempirepublishers.co.uk/

Our books may be purchased in bulk for promotional, educational, or business use.

Please contact The Empire Publishers at +44 20 4579 8116, or by email at support@theempirepublishers.co.uk

First Edition 2025

Paperback ISBN: 978-1-970463-06-4
Hardcover ISBN: 978-1-970463-07-1

i

Dedication

To my Mother and Husband, the two people who carried me when I couldn't walk.

Acknowledgement

I would like to thank The Empire Publishers for all their help and support throughout this whole process. I would also like to thank my creative writing group, Years Ahead, for all the support given while polishing my writing skills. To my Mum, thank you for your love, patience, and support with my writing, and long before I ever picked up a pen. Thank you to my husband, who has stood by me for the last 20 years.

About the Author

Welcome to the debut poetry book from Chel O'Hare, who currently lives in the north of England. She began writing poetry as a therapeutic way of dealing with mental health issues. She has been an active member of a local writing group for the last few years. She also gets a lot of enjoyment from writing *children's* books. She is a keen crafter and loves being at home, where she is married with two sons, five cats, and two guinea pigs.

Contents

Addiction

This was fun at first; I was in complete control.
Now it feels like I've stepped into a manhole.
I'm falling fast — I can't keep up anymore.
Fun shouldn't feel like this, for sure.

People are saying I need to stop right away,
But it's already a problem, and it's here to stay.
I hide it mostly from family and friends,
But unfortunately, this isn't where the story ends.

The compulsion grows bigger by the day,
The debts get higher — it's here to stay.
I can't afford to keep this going,
But somehow I'll find a way to keep playing.
I just wish it would all go away.

Admitting it's a problem is the biggest hurdle.
Saying it out loud makes your stomach curdle.
Taking the first step toward recovery
Will make you feel proud — just wait and see.
Don't give up if you stumble along the way;
It's never your final judgment day.

Staying on track isn't just for today.
It's a lifetime commitment to stay away.
It's easier to have someone along the way,
Someone to check in with so you don't stray.
You don't need someone to hold your hand —
Just someone who listens, who understands.

Addiction can come in many forms;
Each one has its own unique storms:
Gambling, alcohol, drugs, and more —
Each one capable of cutting to your core.
Never feel guilty for having an addiction;
You didn't ask for this affliction.

ADHD

I try to fit in, but you won't give me a chance.
It's not my fault I like to prance.
My thoughts move too quickly for me to keep up;
I feel like an overflowing cup.

People are always shouting my name,
Always quick to point and blame.
I hide under the table in a crowd,
Because the noise is just too loud.

"Unteachable" is a mean thing to say
When I'm just trying to express myself my own way.
With an empty desk in the hall,
You make me feel so very small.

I long to run, dance, and play,
But you just force me to sit still and stay.
You send me home when I express myself,
So I sit quiet, like I've been put on a shelf.

My temper gets the best of me —
I can't control it, honestly.
The days are long and hard to cope;
You're expecting me to climb an uphill slope.

The punishments come thick and fast.
The praise is never here to last.
I'm trying hard each and every day
Just so you might let me stay.

If you look longer and harder at me,
You'll see much more than my ADHD.

I'm growing now; I'm in my teens.
It's not my fault — it's in my genes.
I manage better; I've come so far.
To Mum and Dad, I'm an ADHD superstar.

I fit in now — someone gave me a chance.
There's nothing wrong with wanting to prance.
My thoughts still move super fast,
But now I've learned how to last.

I'm better in a crowd,
Though I cover my ears if it's too loud.
I'm teachable — I'm here to stay.
I'm finally me, in my own way.

A class full of students all sat round —
To be part of this, I feel so proud.
There's a place called "the cloud" where I sit
When I get the feeling I just don't fit.

My temper's fiery; it glows bright red.
But now I control it mostly in my head.
The days are short; so much to see.
I'm just rocking life, being me.

The punishments are few and far between —
Hardly ever a red mark to be seen.
I still try hard every day.
Now I understand I'm not going away.

It's such a small part of the overall me.
Now people see *me*, not just the ADHD.

Broken Earth

The Earth is burning somewhere, but it's far away.
Don't ignore the problem — it's heading your way.
There are dark warnings of what's to come,
But it won't affect our generation, so we play dumb.

Our children's children will gasp for breath.
We'll poison the air until breathing means death.
We're pushing the Earth past the point of no return.
It's getting hotter — it's going to burn.

The storms are stronger; the death count climbs.
We lose track of numbers in these troubled times.
The sea is rising; we're losing ground.
No one listened to thoughts profound.

So much plastic, killing all our fish —
They'd choose life if only they could wish.
Savage hunters kill for fun;
Once an animal's gone, it can't be undone.

Leveling the rainforest miles at a time —
There won't be any left for children to climb.
Building bombs bigger and bigger —
Dangerous people with their hands on the trigger.

So much war with no end in sight.
Why must everything be solved with a fight?
So much suffering from young to old;
We've forgotten our manners — we won't be told.

If we stay on the path we've chosen to take,
We'll keep bending the rules until they break.
A planet at the point of too far gone —
Where will we go when it's no longer safe to stay on?

The future will be a story of days long past,
An Earth that was wonderful before damage too vast.
What will be left when we're done salting the Earth?
We'll be sorry when it's too late for rebirth.

Our planet, broken, just a rock in space —
Will we have enough warning for one last embrace?

We could have lived on this Earth forever,
But we chose to destroy it — however.

Dead Inside

Today's the day I died; you sat back as I cried and cried.
From deep inside I was consumed by despair;
You made no effort to repair.

A scream ripped me apart —
You took, then destroyed, my heart.
I no longer feel anything but pain;
My sanity flushed down the drain.

You've drawn me so close to violence;
You taught me to suffer in silence.
I can't stand you being near,
But when you're gone, there's intense fear.

I can no longer stand on my own —
You've worn my confidence to the bone.
I stand here, an empty shell;
You've locked me in a solitary hell.

I see myself fading away;
I wish you'd give me a reason to stay —
A hint that I mattered.
I gave you my heart, and it shattered.

You promised me forever.
It was a lie, however.
Now I'm curled up alone,
The fate of my life unknown.

I'm balancing on a knife's edge;
I'm afraid I'm too close to the ledge.
I begged you to pull me back.
I see nothing around me but black.

How can you just walk away?
I'm scared I'm starting to decay.
I'd give anything to not be a shell,
Even if it means landing in hell.

I'll pull you down here with me;
You'll never get free.
We'll rot together, just us two.
Watching your soul die will be a plus.

Devil Inside

The devil got into you; I've thought this through.
He seeped into your soul — wherever he found a hole.
He made you quite the maniac;
He turned your insides black.

He'll make you do his bidding,
All your good thoughts forbidding.
He'll make you maim and kill
Until the beast inside you's had its fill.

He'll twist your point of view
Until your thoughts are all askew.
Your thoughts shift, your mind drifts.
Your veins flow dark; your good side lifts.

You start to enjoy the evil;
It makes you feel primeval.
You seek out pure souls
And leave them in empty holes.

You feel your rise to power;
You make the poor ones cower.
But people will band against you,
Gather and slew.

The mass will fight to end your reign,
To free the world from your pain.
They'll battle hard, they won't be swayed,
Until that evil's been repaid.

Your soul will slip to hell;
You'll hear that death bell.
A thousand years of torture,
A lifetime's scorcher.

You can beg for mercy,
But you caused the controversy.
You killed and maimed for fun —
Now your thousand years have begun.

Do You Trust Me?

Do you trust me? I asked as I lay you on my chest.
Do you trust me? I asked, knowing I'd give you nothing but the best.
Do you trust me? I asked as I dipped you in the water you hate.
Do you trust me? I asked as I sat you up straight.

Do you trust me? I asked as I held out my hand.
Do you trust me? I asked as I helped you to stand.

I trust you, Mummy, to keep me steady.
I trust you, Mummy, to help get me ready.
I trust you, Mummy, to keep me safe in the bath.
I trust you, Mummy, to always make me laugh.

I trust you, Mummy, to keep me safe.
I trust you, Mummy, to show me my faith.

Do I trust you, my child, to help me more?
Do I trust you, my child, to help me to the store?
Do I trust you, my child, to visit me all the time?
Do I trust you, my child, to carry on our family line?

Do I trust you, my child, to find me a good home?
Do I trust you, my child, to never leave me alone?

Do we trust each other to always tell the truth?
Do we trust each other to never be aloof?
Do we trust each other to always care?
Do we trust each other to always be there?

Do we trust each other to go the extra mile?
Do we love each other enough to always make each other smile?

Don't Panic

I can see you struggling over there.
You're panicking, but it's okay — I'm here to share.
You're struggling to breathe; I know you're scared.
But I can talk you through this — just let me be heard.

You need to breathe really slow.
We'll count to three, then give it a go.

Hold my hand — we'll see this through.
Just try to focus on me and you.
Your mind is racing; you can't slow it down.
It doesn't feel like it, but you're not going to drown.

Keep focusing on my voice.
You can control this — you have a choice.
You've been here before; you know the score.
Please let me help — don't run out the door.

You've nearly got this, I can tell.
Believe me — you're doing well.
Your breathing's slowing — the end's in sight.
Look at you go — you've won this fight.

Remember when your breathing gets fast:
It's okay to be scared; it won't last.
Have a safety plan, keep it near.
If you're caught out again, it'll help others steer.

Each one feels worse than the last,
But you're getting through them, faster and faster.

Doubt

I wasn't born — I was cleverly created
From everything dark that people hated.
I was dragged into you from the start,
With the power to pull your world apart.

A disease sent to wander the earth,
To steal your pride and self-worth.
No force was made to keep me down;
My emptiness could make you drown.

My goal on earth was always clear:
To cause endless, pointless fear.
I don't face your weakness —
I bring constant bleakness.

I'm the shadow in the dark that you fear.
I'm the evil you hate to have near.
I crawl deep under your skin,
Inside your head, I'll make a din.

I make you second-guess every move.
Impossible to forget or remove.
I sit back and admire my work,
Taunting you with a nasty smirk.

My job's to make you question your mind.
I never claimed to be fair or kind.
So many cry alone —
I think I've earned my throne.

No one keeps me away —
Try all you want; I always stay.
I chip at your sanity,
Till you're embarrassed by your vanity.

Don't think daily prayer will make me stray.
I'll be waiting in your nightmare's gray.
You'll accept me, but we'll never be friends.
I'm the thing your mind can't comprehend.

I'll keep you from moving too far —
I'm always there, like a scar.

If you're still unsure what I'm about,
Silly child — they call me Doubt.

Emotions

When all your emotions are hitting you again and again,
With such force, they cause physical pain,
All mixed up and so tightly combined—
An impossible task to try and unwind.
Stop. Don't panic. I'm here for you.
Let's talk your feelings through.

First, you're crying—what's wrong?
Let's start here and help you feel strong.
I can't make your troubles go away,
But I promise, until you're well, I'm here to stay.
Start right at the beginning.
Take it slow, or your head will start spinning.

Next, you're panicking—but that's okay.
We'll breathe together. I know the way.
Step by step, we'll calm you down.
I promise you, you won't drown.
Breathe one breath at a time.
It's going to feel like an uphill climb.

You're feeling frustrated—I can see why.
When nothing changes, no matter how hard you try.
Don't give up. Don't stop trying.
There's nothing wrong with crying.
Go back to your breath—in and out.
When I'm frustrated, I sometimes shout.

I can see anger in your face.
Slow down—put your anger in its place.
Ask it questions. Find out why it stays.
You can process it in healthier ways.
Tell it it has to step aside—
To let other emotions come through inside.

You're moving forward—be proud of you.
Together, we'll sort your emotions through.
It's not going to be easy every time.
Going slow is never a crime.
Keep focusing—don't push emotions aside.
They'll come and go, just like the tide.

Fairy Tale

I'm here in a place where I belong—my destiny—
A place where every word is a song.
Where the sun always shines and the birds always sing,
And Prince Charming waits on bended knee with a ring.

My heart is new, with not a scar in sight;
It will never know the pain of a lover's fight.
They will write stories of our love through the ages—
Our masterpiece, our tale, penned on golden pages.

They'll speak of the king who found his queen,
And gave her a love so pure, so serene.
The king speaks words they long to hear—
A love song in every note, each word sincere.

The perfect melody plays in the air without end,
The purest emotion with no need to pretend.
They copy us dancing through every storm,
Always in step, with flawless form.

A love that shines brighter than all the stars—
It's perfect, it's beautiful, and it's all ours.
Fireworks light the sky with each perfect kiss;
Time stands still in eternal bliss.

They try to imitate the bond we share—
A deep, everlasting love so rare.
Even the sunset was made to resemble
A love so powerful, it makes lovers tremble.

Flashbacks

I can see the panic in your eyes—
Flashbacks can come as quite a surprise.
It makes no sense—one minute you're great,
The next, you simply can't concentrate.

All your senses kick in at once,
And you can no longer form a response.

Your mind throws you back to that very place—
The one you've spent so long trying not to face.
It haunts your dreams almost every night,
Until falling asleep becomes a fright.

Voices and visions become the norm
While you're still fighting through your storm.

Smells and noises strike like a slap to the face,
Not allowing you to set the pace.
They hit you with the force of a tidal wave—
You're consumed, you've become the nightmare's slave.

Shouting and screaming as the flashback feels real—
Sometimes all we need is space to heal.

Try to step back—it's only a feeling.
Each one you face brings you closer to healing.
Try to ground yourself in the moment—
You don't want to become your own opponent.

Tell your mind: you're safe where you're at.
Your brain plays tricks—it's good at that.

Grounding helps: try counting one to five—
Five things you can see; easy to survive.
Four things you can touch—
It's not asking for too much.

Three things you can hear—
Let's shift this up a gear.
Two things you can smell—
Keep going, you're doing so well.

One thing you can taste—
Take your time, there's no need for haste.

Now the moment has passed; it's gone at last.
Give yourself a cheer—there's nothing to fear.
You'll get stronger after each time.
Look at you—you're starting to climb.

Always remember: count one to five.
In that moment, it will help you survive.

For My Mum

I thought you knew what was in my head—
I suppose it left quite a lot unsaid.
You've been my teacher from the very start,
The first person I kept safe in my heart.

We've been on a journey all my life—
You were rock-solid through all my strife.
I learned so much from watching you;
You knew when to explain and guide me through.

You let me make my own mistakes,
To learn and grow—whatever it takes.
"Mum knows everything," you used to say.
I could count on you to show me the way.

I never doubted you were strong enough—
You were always fair, and never too tough.
I can look back at my life and smile—
You really went that extra mile.

You hold a place no one else could start—
You were there at the very heart.
I feel such pride when I think of you,
I know for sure there's nothing you couldn't do.

You have an inner strength that glows—
I love you, Mum, and I hope everyone knows.

I'll always follow the steps you carved for me—
It's how I guide my children, as you can see.
I want to give them the love you showed—
The kind of love that always glowed.

I'm the man I am because of you—
You held me steady and helped me through.
I still reach for your hand when the moment calls—
An unspoken love that never falls.

I'll never need to look far to see your face—
You're my only Mum—one I could never replace.
Your light will guide me as long as I walk this earth—
There's not enough gold to measure your worth.

Goodbye

Don't say that word—I don't want to hear.
Please don't leave me; I need you near.
I know you never promised me the world,
But after all this time, I thought you cared.

You told me I could be honest with you,
Then walked away—I knew you wouldn't see it through.
Every time you said it would be okay,
You already knew you weren't going to stay.

You knocked down my wall, bit by bit,
Then chipped at my armour until it no longer fit.
You exposed my feelings and set them free,
Then turned your back as I fell to my knee.

You left me broken, lying in the dirt—
I never saw it coming or knew how much it would hurt.
I never realised what you meant to me
Until the moment you chose to set me free.

My armour is back, my wall freshly laid—
But I'll never move on… because you never stayed.

Hate

We'll open up a space for you to look in—
But beware, you'll fall inside before you see the sin.
There's a production line making only anger and hate,
We lure you in with rose-tainted bait.

Take a tour, guided through our twisted halls,
But all you'll find is where happiness falls.
A colourful firework explodes in your face—
Heat and pain, then vanishes without trace.

We love the many colours that burst and break,
It entertains the part of us that wants to watch you ache.
There's a cannonball aimed at where it hurts,
We watch your mind twist, we savour the perverts.

Losing control is our greatest delight—
We scar your sanity and drain your fight.
We watch your claw marks with wicked glee,
You should've paid heed to our one guarantee.

This quirky place where torment thrives—
Where all that was good packed up and left our lives.
We spark the flame and let it grow,
You fan it further and fuel the show.

A nudge to tease out all your wrath,
There's only pain at the end of this path.
One way in and no way out—
We'll laugh as long as you still shout.

We hold the loudest explosion—we'll give it to you,
It'll crush your joy before it's through.
Our words are twisted, never clear,
We amplify pain while feeding your fear.

You can join in our hate—learn to despise—
Or suffer your fate with shattered ties.
We dig in deep and never release—
We thrive while you beg for peace.

We're a force you can't fight, as old as the night,
Down here you'll forget all that was light.

And though we fill you with shame and flame,
I truly don't care if I take all the blame.

Hope's Dead

I remember when you handed me the earth,
Said there was no sum that could match my worth.
I thought I was finally free—
That you'd saved me from the worst of me.

You promised you'd always try,
That you'd never be the reason I cry.
You said you were strong enough for us both,
Your forever-love sealed with an oath.

My future looked so clear—
Everything I'd ever need was here.
We made our plans side by side,
Ready for every storm and tide.

But soon the doubts began to creep,
Our conversations turned from calm to deep.
I started to wonder if I was enough—
Why did loving me feel so tough?

I remember the first time I cried—
It felt like something inside me had died.
The road ahead blurred in the mist,
I forgot the last time you leaned in to kiss.

Could this be falling apart?
What now becomes of my heart?
Can someone survive this endless rain?
Can someone endure this much pain?

I'm silently screaming deep inside—
I've lost count of the times I've tried.
You don't hear my pleas anymore—
You turned my dream into a war.

There's no more fight left in me—
You've crushed my spirit completely.
I shouldn't have trusted your lies—
You never once helped silence my cries.

Each night is a storm of dread—
No strength remains to lift my head.

It's chaos now—this mess inside.
And a lifetime to learn how to hide.

I Hate You

Lost on a path called "Keep it Together"—
This relationship's light as a feather.
How long can I fake this smile?
Honestly, it's been fake for quite a while.

I list the good and bad in my mind—
But one side's long, the other's hard to find.
I wish I could take a break from you—
I'm tired of this same, toxic view.

This turned toxic some time ago,
I'm sick of pretending for show.
I can't say when I began to hate your face,
But now I need my own safe space.

We're bound by something I can't undo—
But I'm close to being done with you.
The only thing that gets me through the day,
Is knowing I'm helping your joy decay.

I get a thrill from watching you fall—
You deserve each moment I made you feel small.
I'll laugh the day I push you to the edge—
Even better if it's off a ledge.

The hatred now is starting to burn,
My only concern is not letting it churn.
I show the world there's nothing wrong—
Smiling outside while seething strong.

I can't recall what came before—
I locked us both inside a darkened door.
I filled it with flowers sharp with pain,
Each petal meant to drive you insane.

I make you bleed, inside and out—
And no one hears you when you shout.
It begins and ends with all my hate—
I've sealed you into a cruel fate.

Now I'm alone in this room I built—
So much rage, so much guilt.

I've waged this war to tear us apart—
And I've got direct access to your heart.

I Need You

It hurts when I breathe at the thought you might leave,
The void you'd leave behind—I can't conceive.
Your soul swallowed mine, whole and wide—
Was that your endgame, or something you hide?

A tug of war we play each day—
Will you go, or will you stay?
I need to know you're here to stay,
I can't live any other way.

It's all or nothing—that's the cost.
My self-worth is getting lost.

So many years I've clung so tight—
Wishing you'd never vanish from sight.
Please don't leave me all alone—
I'll raise you up, I'll build a throne.

I'll worship you if that's what it takes,
I'll write my truth in poems and aches.
For you to want me like I want you—
It's too late now to withdraw or undo.

We're tied together—forever, it seems—
Bound by children and fractured dreams.

I can't live without you, though I wish you knew.
I think you feel the same way too.
Invisible strings keep us near—
We could shine through storm and fear.

If you still need me like I need you,
This blip is something we can work through.
I'll give you time if you'll teach me to shine.
Please—I'm begging. Don't cross that line.

When I Think of You

When the morning sky turns purple and pink,
And I could stare for hours, barely blink—
I'll think of you.

When spring days stretch a little longer,
And the sun's warmth grows a little stronger—
I'll think of you.

When we gather in gardens with laughter and friends,
And hope the joy never ends—
I'll think of you.

When I see a smile, genuine and true,
I'll remember how beautiful yours was too—
I'll think of you.

And when we sit and reflect on life's view,
Knowing there's one more star shining through—
I'll think of you.

Life

Not everything lasts forever; the world goes on, regardless, however.
You can cherish every flower, but it wilts despite your power.
Everything has an end—of this, you can depend.
There's not always a chance to say goodbye, even though we always try.
You can't stop things from naturally dying, no matter how much you're really trying.
There's lots to gain by letting go—this is a lesson life will always show.

You can't hold on to the past; life moves on much too fast.
There's little point in looking back—it's when you turn your back that wolves attack.
Keep yourself pointed straight; the horse has bolted, so why close the gate?
Never cling to what has gone; move out of the past to where the sun has shone.
There's a good reason why things get left behind: so the future isn't just as blind.
Don't hold onto memories too tight—they can be deceptive and not worth the fight.

There's lots to gain by moving on; accept a little push when the safety's gone.
Accept nothing but the very best—life teaches you this with its little tests.
Hold on tight to those you love; life's too short to push and shove.
Stand up tall and straighten your crown—then stand and watch who starts to frown.
Loyalty is life's main key; hold it tight—it will set your soul free.
Don't be tied down to bad feelings; let them go and start your healing.

Make a Difference

We only get a tiny moment of space,
Our lives—they leave hardly any trace.
We all want to leave our own footprint,
That we were here, maybe just a hint.
We want to leave a mark, show we were here,
Do something daring, and have no fear.

Save the ocean or save the bees,
Do something heroic like save the trees.
Stop the polar ice from melting—
Anything, as long as we think we're helping.
Save the dogs and save the cats;
Let's not leave it up to bureaucrats.

We make no impact while we are on our own,
But as a force together, it has been shown.
Let's join hands and stand side by side;
If we're loud enough, our voices they can't hide.
We'll shout for peace, end hunger or strife—
That's how we make an impact in our life.

Stand tall, and demand your place in time.
Let us do this now, while in our prime.
Leave your mark and make it deep;
Don't go through your life fast asleep.
Make your life well worth living—
Don't leave your mark as only wishing.

Light at the End of the Tunnel

I have a question, please, do you know?
I need to be started on the right way to go.
I'm searching for a tunnel, it's one I've seen before.
Last time I saw it, it was behind a white door.
I dream of getting to the tunnel every night.
It's time I had it in my sight.
If you want, I'll tell you what's inside.
It's a place where hope likes to hide.
I dream of a light inside that is just out of reach,
But that light, when caught, has much to teach.
It's the brightest light, though it looks quite small.
It pulls me in, but I've always been afraid I'll fall.

This light is magic, it can heal my pain.
It can pull me to a place where there's no more rain.
If I move slowly and grab firmly to that light,
I know there's a world where it's always bright.
I watch in amazement as the light gets bigger all the time,
Whispering softly that happiness isn't a crime.
The tunnel is long, I've seen it, I know,
But through the tunnel is the way to go.
The light becomes dazzling, it's pure and bright.
It has the power to banish the night.
A feeling of warmth I'd long since forgot,
I remember I like the feeling a lot.

This tunnel is there, now I'm ready to pass.
My peace of mind is no longer shards of glass.
I can walk with confidence to the end and see,
There's so much joy in being free.
The light, it doesn't stop at the end.
It moves inside your heart like a treasured friend.
I'll leave a map for others to follow,
To show them there's a tunnel that's long and hollow.
They'll follow my steps and the path that I chose,
A path of discovery, I suppose.
At the end of the tunnel is a wondrous light—
At last, a life so stunningly bright.

Better the Devil You Know

You pulled my world from under my feet.
You stamped on my heart without missing a beat.
I can't believe I never saw it before.
You were always mine but had a foot out the door.
I'm stood here, scared, facing a new day,
Unsure if there's any reason left to stay.
You promised a world dripping in bliss.
I can't believe it's come down to this.
Is there anything left in this life for me?
I've really tried, but there's nothing I can see.
I'll never get back what you took from me.
I'm drowning in enough tears to fill the sea.

You killed me from inside and made it slow.
You taught me to never let it show.
I thought it was me that had caused this mess.
That's how you wanted it, though, I guess.
You twisted and pulled me deep inside,
Then walked away whenever I cried.
You often made me doubt my own mind.
Then in front of others, it was sympathy and kind.
I often wonder if you'll ever fall.
Do you even feel anything at all?
When did your heart turn to stone?
You walked out the door and left me all alone.

I'll wait forever to see the tables turning.
The fire in me will always be burning.
You sentenced me to a living hell—
An empty, discarded, broken shell.
I'll never recover what you took from me.
You'd have seen me in hell before you set me free.
Was I destined to be your game?
I can never leave with all this shame.
There's nothing really left of me now.
My heart resembles something that's been through a plough.
You know I'll still stay with you forever.
Broken together is better than alone, however.

My Holiday

It's 2004, I'm boarding a plane.
I'm travelling alone—I must be insane.
I'm in Indonesia for a Christmas break.
I'm not aware there's a far-off quake.
I see the sea run far from me.
I'm quite confused; it's a sight to see.
I see everyone stop with a frown on their face.
Why is the sea no longer in its place?
The sea's returning—people start to scream.
I hope this is just a nasty dream.
I'm standing frozen, I can't deny.
I think that wave is thirty foot high.

I've no more time to run and hide.
It's above my head, about to collide.
This pain I'm feeling as the wave crashes down,
Relentlessly flinging me through the town.
It's so much more than I think I can bear.
There's nothing on earth that will compare.
I'm trying so hard to stay afloat.
There's too much water in my throat.
I can see nothing but water and people in distress—
Blood and death, it's such a mess.
Will this endless flow of water stop?
What will be left when the levels drop?

The water has gone; I'm too scared to look around.
Manic crying is the only sound.
Boxing Day is over and people start to count—
One hundred and three thousand is Indonesia's amount.
Will this world ever be the same?
Two hundred and thirty thousand dead, but no one to blame.
I'm still standing; I don't know where to start.
This broken land I don't want to depart.
I'm here to stay, and I'll stay till it's fixed.
With sadness and determination, my feelings are mixed.
Here is my story for you to retell—
Of this holiday that came straight from hell.

My Strength

My mind takes me places I don't want to go,
And my eyes see things I don't want them to show.
I fear the things that aren't really there.
Sometimes it's almost too much to bear.
Standing close but never in the way,
You tell me it's all going to be okay.
I hear your voice when the sound is deafening.
I can follow it back like it's beckoning.
I've searched for years for a place I could be strong.
How could I have missed you were my safe place all along?
I turn to you because you've never lied.
I'm as sure of you as I am of the tide.

I'm often confused by the view.
It makes more sense when you talk it through.
There's a lot I don't understand.
You explained why I had to learn to stand.
Things get so mixed till my head spins.
You help me control it from when it begins.
It's been a long road, but I never walked alone.
You're the strongest person I've ever known.
I never felt you pulling back.
You always get me back on track.
You make my world crystal clear.
I can take on the world when you're near.

I see so much strength when I look at you.
It's because of that strength I finally grew.
You teach me it's never too late to learn.
Everyone eventually gets their turn.
You're determined and strong; you know your mind,
But it's never done by being unkind.
You understand me without a sound.
You easily pick me up off the ground.
I never question needing you.
Whatever it is, you'll see me through.
My greatest wish is to be just like you.
It's what I live up to do.

Overwhelmed

I'm overwhelmed, I cannot cope.
At this moment, I feel no hope.
My emotions are taking me for a ride.
This bursting feeling I cannot hide.
It overflowed, and now it's out.
I feel the need to really shout.

I know addiction is my own doing,
But this is a new path that I'm pursuing.
I know you want to help me on my way,
But I must find my own path at the end of the day.
I got myself into this mess.
I'm trying to deal with all the stress.

It's not as easy as it looks.
You won't find the answer in any books.
I need to draw strength from deep inside.
I've got so many demons trying to hide.
There's no straight path, I might occasionally fail.
You can't then put me in an emotional jail.

I'll pick myself up and start again.
I don't deliberately over complain.
I have more issues than most people do.
It's just a knock-on from what I've been through.
I know I sometimes overshare.
I'm just looking for confirmation that you care.

I feel the need to have some space.
I can't keep up with life at this pace.
I'm struggling now, I'm asking for time.
My life, it runs like a pantomime.
I need to slow things right down.
I don't want to be in the middle of this meltdown.

Questions

If I smile at you, would you smile at me?
Would you smile openly for all to see?
If you smiled at me and everyone saw,
Would you quickly hide behind the door?
Let us go outside and put it to the test.
We'll smile at each other and ignore the rest.

If I spoke to you, would you speak to me?
Would you talk out loud for all to see?
If you spoke to me and everyone saw,
Would you turn your voice into a roar?
Let us move about and speak out loud.
We'll speak to each other and sound so proud.

If I held your hand, would you hold mine?
Would you hold it very strong and long?
If you held my hand and everyone saw,
Would you keep a tight grip like it was a law?
Let us walk around without a sound.
We'll hold hands with each other, then move on to another.

If I hugged you tight, would you hug me back?
Would you hold on with all your might?
If you hugged me tight and everyone saw,
Would you keep on hugging until I thaw?
Let us stand on a hill up high
And hug each other till we die.

If I said I loved you, would the words be mine?
Would you say it loud and just in time?
If you said you loved me and everyone saw,
Would you hold me together like a jigsaw?
Let us say the words for the world to hear
And keep each other very near.

Thank You

I'm always thinking life's just too hard,
That maybe I'm just too badly scarred.
I'm always thinking about the past.
I never really noticed time was going by so fast.
I walk around blindly, feeling confused.
Can't shake the feeling that I'm too badly used.
I kill any happiness that dares come my way,
But I'll keep and nurture any dismay.
I guess life is what you make of it.
I made it black, I'll have to admit.
I pushed away everyone who brought me light.
I only exist deep in the night.

You never tried to push me too hard.
I don't think you even noticed I was scarred.
You never let me sit with the past.
You taught me to hold on when life got fast.
You said it was okay to get confused,
That I was too special to be classed as used.
You showed me how to nurture any happiness that came my way,
And kill all those feelings of dismay.
You knew life is what you make of it.
You filled mine with colour, I'll have to admit.
You pulled in so much of the bright light—
Bright enough to banish the night.

Together we smashed through the hard.
I've almost forgotten I was ever scarred.
Together we can briefly visit the past.
I now know how to leave there really fast.
Together we have each other if we get confused.
How could I ever think I was used?
Together we welcome all happiness our way.
We're far too happy for dismay.
Together this is a good life we made of it,
Overflowing with colours, I'm pleased to admit.
Together we shine the brightest light.
I can't even remember what it looks like at night.

The Baby Bird

I was walking through the wood, doing nothing that I should,
When I nearly stepped on a baby bird that I only faintly heard.
It was a bird I'd never seen before,
It was magnificent, for sure.
Its colours were quite magical,
Its form quite classical.
I knew this bird was special—pure friendship in this vessel.
I gently picked it up from the ground, eager to see what I had found.

I cared for and nurtured the tiny bird, never feeling scared.
For the friendship that it brought me, I couldn't wait to see.
It would be full of sharing, always there when we needed caring.
A true friend I could confide in, where I wouldn't have to hide my sin.
Days out to fun places—we wouldn't need airs and graces.
A bond that could never be spoken, or leave you heartbroken.

That bird, it grew fast, its colours quite contrast.
It grew strong and fast—far too fast to last.
It became so intense, it no longer made any sense.
That bird, it flew through the sky, a friendship you could certify.
But the bird was slowing down, the friends were starting to frown.
The bird had had its day; the friendship started to decay.

As the bird's magical colour faded, the friendship found it hadn't made it.
The bird wasn't for much more time; the friendship had also lost its shine.
The bird stopped flying—it was much too weak.
The friendship was long past its peak.
There was no more time to make it shine—
They were both elsewhere, having a good time.
The friendship and bird decayed together.
No one promised it would last forever.
I said goodbye to my little bird,
And the friendship it incurred.

The Big Outdoors

When it's been such a long time since you've been outside,
When the thought of the door makes you want to hide,
Stop and breathe, take it one step at a time,
Try not to focus on the end of the climb.
Step by step, we'll do this together,
I'll support you, no matter the weather.

Get yourself ready, we're walking to the door.
We're not going out yet, you can be sure.
Just getting to the door is a huge thing,
We'll soon have you confident enough to sing.
Walk all around by the door;
This will boost your confidence for sure.

Next, a big step, we're going to open the door.
Breathe slow, keep your feet on the floor.
Stand by the door, take a look around,
You can see there's no fear to be found.
You're panicking now, hold my hand.
You feel like your breath is restricted by a band.

Finally, you try stepping outside into fresh air.
This is a huge moment we can share.
No one is asking you to start to run,
Just stand by the door and enjoy the sun.
When you're ready, put one foot in front of the other,
You'll be amazed how much ground you can cover.

Take each step, one at a time,
Repeating a step isn't a crime.
Go at a pace that works for you,
You'll soon have a whole new world view.
This is your time, this is your cue,
Take control and do it for you.

The Grim Reaper

Let's take this slowly, we'll go at your pace,
This isn't the time to panic and race.
I'm here for you now, it's just you and me,
We've got all the time in the world, you see.
Don't be too scared of the things that you've heard,
Just follow me slowly, feel free to stay near.
I'll make your journey crystal clear.

I'm not here to judge your journey or path,
It's not my place to show kindness or wrath.
Your life, good or bad, doesn't alter this road,
I'm just here to guide you out of the cold.
We walk in silence, there's nothing to say,
You run out of words on your final day.

We'll keep on walking till you're no longer scared,
My only job is to get you prepared.
This road is one we all must take,
But at the right time, I'll never forsake.
We're getting closer, you won't need my hand,
As you take your first steps on your new land.

I'll leave you now, my job here is done,
You're finally at peace in the endless sun.
There is no fear in this perfect place,
The peace is endless, there is no race.
I must go back, someone else needs me now,
I'll leave you with God as you take a bow.

The Light Through the Window

There's a blackened window in my room, what lies beyond I can only assume.
In the corner, a light breaks through, just not enough to see the view.
My thoughts, they focus on this light, what lies beyond must be quite the sight.
A single tear runs down my face, I long to see a brighter place.
I have a thousand thoughts, each one intense,
But in my mind they don't make sense.
I long and pray to touch the light,
To move away from this endless night.

I try so hard to tear the darkness away,
I feel my mind begin to decay.
I rub my hand across my neck,
I wish the light was more than just a speck.
Is my happiness beyond that windowpane?
I try so hard, but it's all in vain.
I'm often too scared to move or speak,
The fear inside has left me weak.
I reach out with the last of my strength,
To touch the light I'd go to any length.
I feel a gentle warmth on my hand,
It gives me the strength to finally stand.

The light grows slightly, it gets warmer still,
I'm so excited, it's such a thrill.
My other arm reaches out,
I can do this, I have no doubt.
I grab the dark and rip it away,
This is my time, now, today.
The warmth moves inside me, I'm so close to being free.
The view is stunning, my eyes open wide,
Imagine if I hadn't tried.
The light's inside, only I can take it away,
Now I've felt the warmth, I'll let it stay.

The Maze

Welcome to my mind, you'll find it's quite the maze.
Don't be alarmed, but it's where the madness stays.
The paths are long and full of turns,
There's no one sane to hear your concerns.

Every path you follow leads to endless dead ends,
You'll chase your own sanity round the endless bends.
You'll meet strange people on the way,
I'm fairly sure they're only there to play.

You'll stumble and trip on my issues,
When you lose your mind, we'll provide comforting tissues.
Keep moving and never stop for too long,
You'll eventually find yourself starting to belong.

The maze is long, its walls are high,
It amuses me to watch you cry.
Along the way, you'll see disturbing sights.
When you've seen them too long, they become delights.

I've lined the maze with doom and gloom,
A touch of negativity wherever I found room.
If you make it through, you'll never come back.
My twisted mind will give you quite the whack.

Bring your friends and explore my madness.
Take a wrong turn and you'll face my sadness.
Keep on walking and feel free to shout,
You'll soon find out there's no way out.

My maze of madness is scarily outrageous.
Just as scary is it's really contagious.
There's a pit in the middle, don't fall down.
There's enough demons in there to make you drown.

Keep out the shadows, they'll swallow you whole,
But you can bargain out if you surrender your soul.
You'll soon give up the will to fight,
My eternal madness dripping in spite.

You'll start to doubt everything you see.
Try as you might, there's nowhere to flee.

You're always welcome to come inside.
It makes for one hell of a ride.

The Ultimate Climb

I finally hit rock bottom, I couldn't go any lower.
Down at rock bottom, life is always much slower.
I finally found my feet and shook off the dust.
I didn't realise I was gathering so much rust.
I looked up warily to find the light,
Amazed that it was coming from such a height.

I dug my hands hard into the wall,
No longer afraid that I will always fall.
I gripped on hard, with all my might,
And carved a hole to hold on tight.
I heaved myself up to the first of many holes.
This time I wasn't letting go till I reached my goals.

Determination pushing me up toward the light,
Could my new beginning really be in sight?
On the way up there were rocks to avoid.
I'm feeling too enlightened to be annoyed.
This twisted wall that I must climb
Won't let you stop and rest for half-time.

With a firm hold, I reach the top of my wall.
I pull myself up and stand really tall.
I look around for my new direction, then I realised:
It's a new path I want, my old one I'd out-sized.
I feel powerful and strong, my life a brand new beginning.
I'm a force of positivity, and it's got me grinning.

I did it, I'm free, no more wounds you can see.
I'll take life's best hand and fly because I'm free.
I'm a new force of nature, my life mine to own.
I'll make mistakes on the way, but I'll no longer moan.
I'll never look back, there's nothing there left to see.
I'm looking firmly forward, and I'm as proud as can be.

I'm finally happy, my old scars have faded.
There are no longer holes I have to keep shaded.
There is a place in life for everyone to grasp.
Spreading the news is my ultimate task.
I'll spread my secret, then it's your turn to climb.
There's beauty and peace at the top every time.

To Fit In

To live in your world, what must I be?
Subdued and normal, completely delusion-free.
I shape myself so not to stand out.
No one gets more than a glimpse of what I'm about.

Pushed to the shadows, hidden from view,
What's in my mind is a huge taboo.
People want stability to be by my side.
I have lots of emotions I'm taught to hide.

I use my life to see the funny side.
I've done nothing wrong. Why should I hide?
I have to find reasons to get through the day.
This is my life, it's unscripted like a play.

I don't know which me steps forward to react.
It's a rollercoaster ride, that's a fact.
Floating so high, then sinking so low,
It's sometimes easier to go with the flow.

I'm still learning to keep myself together.
I'm as unpredictable as the weather.
The pendulum swings from side to side,
Consistently changing like the tide.

I try to blend in with others around.
People are easy to mimic, I've found.
It's easy to forget who the real me should be.
She's locked inside, never to be free.

To You

I can't comprehend how much I love you,
I know it's forever and true.
From deep in my soul I can feel,
Your voice has the power to heal.

Something sparked a burning flame,
Then an eternal light that flame became.
Never dimming but perfectly bright,
Then a raging fire, to my delight.

Never could I imagine the perfection,
The deep-as-the-sea connection.
The sense that we're meant to be,
Joined by fate but still free.

This journey we're taking together
Has its seasons, just like the weather.
The joy and wonder of spring,
When we became so much more than a fling.

We fell in love in summer, in the heat,
Without you I felt incomplete.
We were so content when autumn set in,
You could still make my head spin.

There was no end in sight through winter,
You'd got under my skin like a splinter.
Our road went on forever,
I couldn't survive if we were to sever.

I finally understood what it meant to live,
My heart I was glad to give.
We can tell each other a story with a glance,
Our endless, beautiful romance.

I believe beauty is in the eye of the beholder,
Your shine for me will never get older.
A story of princesses and magic,
But our story will never end tragic.

We can ground each other through the wildest storm,
The fire inside will keep us warm.

To the end of our days I'll hold you so dear,
You're my soulmate, that is perfectly clear.

With Sympathy

A bottomless feeling of despair,
A small crowd moves in that really cares.
When memories are all that's left,
Each emotion is one of bereft.

Caring hands reach out to you,
Hold them tight and they'll guide you through.
One small step at a time,
This may be your biggest climb.

So many words but none make sense,
The silent scream is so intense.
Each second's a fight just to get by,
She's now on a pedestal way up high.

Take comfort where you can,
You'll always be her biggest fan.
There is always a rainbow after the storm,
After the cold, life will once again be warm.

As you walk through life she'll be by your side,
Always there, filled with pride.
A loving thought, a memory, a smile,
They get easier after a while.

The road ahead, no longer together,
Blown off course just like a feather.
A second to question the rules of life,
Why it handed you so much strife.

In time you'll find a reason to smile,
Remember her ways, remember her style.
A perfect couple destined to be,
It was written in the stars, we all agree.

When two pure souls find themselves entwined,
They will be forever, never confined.
We will hold you strong whenever you need,
Endless support guaranteed.

Take each memory, carve it in stone,
With all of these you'll never be alone.

A love like yours can't just end,
The sadness is too much to comprehend.